TRANSFORMED

The Journey to Becoming

Sabine Gedeon

I dedicate this book to those in my lineage, past, present, and future. May the freedom, healing, glory, power, and manifested grace and restoration of Christ Jesus be unveiled in you!

CONTENTS

INTRODUCTION

From the moment I opened my eyes, to the second I closed them to sleep, I was in a mental hell.

It was the summer of 2007 when it happened; I hit rock bottom! Looking at the decisions I'd made, the people I'd allowed into my life, the behaviors that were killing me from the inside out, I had to finally admit that I didn't love myself. How could I, given the landscape of my life? The truth is, I didn't know what love was back then. I thought it was simply a strong, positive emotion and never having experienced real love ever in my life, I was made to believe that love was painful. The more painful it was, the more I was loved. So naturally, I couldn't recognize or even accept love when it presented itself to me; not because

I didn't want it, but because I didn't know how to receive it.

During this period of extended depression, mental-torment, and hopelessness, I had been working in my field incorporate, while still working part-time at a major retail drug store. For months, from the moment I opened my eyes, to the second I closed them to fall asleep, I was in a mental hell. Thoughts, images, words of hate, words of judgment and insecurity bombarded my mind.

Feelings of regret, disappointment, and self-loathing overwhelmed me to the point I couldn't take it anymore. It didn't matter where I was or what I was doing, the smallest trigger would send me spiraling down the deepest pits of despair. With no one to talk to and no one to trust with this deep wound, I buried all of it inside my heart.

I was so good at being "strong" that I didn't and couldn't let anyone in on my weakness.

I showed up every day with a smile on my face and a gaping hole in my heart. I carried that pain like it was an armor of some sort, so much so, no one around me knew much about the raging battle going on inside of me; the fight taking place for my life and my destiny. It got so bad that I used to get high almost every day and drink alcohol until I had passed out and fallen asleep, just so I could "escape" the demons in my head, constantly telling me and reminding me how much of a "shitty" person I was and had always been, that my entire life, no one really liked me or wanted me around, that I was so desperate to be loved, I just let anyone take advantage of me and my body, I was worthless, I wasn't pretty, and I didn't have much to live for. I was inmy own personal hell in my mind for months and no one even knew. I was so good at being "strong" that I didn't and couldn't let anyone in on my weakness. Not even my sister, who I'd grown really close to, had a clue of what I was dealing with.

After several months of pain and mental torture, I finally decided that the only solution to all of this was to take my life and end the suffering. So that's exactly what I set out to do. I devised a plan to take some pills from the pharmacy I was working part-time. Choosing a night where I didn't have to work, I would say goodbye to the world and finally, put an end to the torture I was going through. This was it, I was moving forward with the plan and no one was going to stop me. I told no one what I was planning and made sure not to give off any hints at work or anywhere else. I would show up for work one day, and the next, I'd be gone forever. Just a distant memory. At that point, my whole life had revolved around pain and happiness, or what others might call a "normal life" seemed outside of my control and so far out of reach for me, this would be my way of finally taking control over my life.

I would show up for work one day, and the next, I'd be gone forever. Just a distant memory.

From the moment I was conceived, pain had claimed a stake on my life and was not going to let go, at least not without a fight. See, I was born into a situation where my mother had just lost a child some months before she found out she was pregnant with me. Having given birth to three sons prior to that time, one being a still-birth, and another dying in her arms on the way to the hospital at the age of one, I suspect she wasn't in the right emotional frame of mind where she could handle or sustain the thought of having another child, much less a daughter; and this was so evident in the way she received and treated me. Coming off the heel of losing an infant unexpectedly, it was brutally obvious to me and everyone around me that she didn't want another child. To make matters even more complicated, shortly after my birth, my mother's residency paperwork was approved, and she was given the green light to come live in the United States permanently. So, by the time I was four months old, I found myself motherless. Luckily, I had an amazing aunt, who was just a teenager herself, to love and nurture me those first few critical months and years. At the time of writing of this book, I don't have kids yet but I have spoken with and been around a good number of new moms, to know the bond they share with their newborns is indescribable. And because the bond between mother and child is so strong, in most cases, they are nearly inseparable. This, of course, is provided there aren't any underlying challenges such as postpartum depression, or other related emotional issues, which my mother could have very well experienced. So it's really not hard or unfair to presume that between the timing of my entry into the world, following the death of my infant brother, and the timing of my mother's departure out of the country, the seeds of abandonment and rejection were fully sown and planted. Anything layered on top of that, which I'll share in more detail later, eventually served as the soil, light and water needed to grow a painful and destructive harvest, otherwise known as my life.

These earlier accounts of my life, coupled with my experience being raised by an emotionally challenged mother, left me feeling and believing that I was unwanted, unloved, and worthless. And although I can't prove the level of emotional scarring that took place in me with scientific data or scripture, I know this for sure, the absence of a mother's love is damaging to one's soul in ways that can never be described or explained. And though my life has been completely transformed and I've been healed on so many levels, it was those earlier scars that brought me to the place of suicide, and the place of lost hope. I'll share more about my childhood experiences throughout the remaining chapters, but for now, just keep the circumstances around my birth into this world in the back of your mind as I take you through my journey of personal transformation.

CHAPTER 1

Standing at Death's Door

After months of pain and mental torture, I finally decided that the only solution to all of this was to take my life and end the suffering.

The night before "the big day" had arrived,and I was scheduled to work at the pharmacy the following day, As I cleaned my apartment and got all my things in order, I found myself taking a break to revisit the plan in my head. I also started replaying events that had taken place throughout my childhood, adolescence, and early adulthood that led up to that unforgettable night. All the heartaches, verbal, emotional, physical, and sexual abuse I'd endured, all the fake friendships I'd entertained as real, and the disappointments.

Then suddenly, I had a flashback of standing in the kitchen of my parent's condo, at the age of 13, with a knife to my wrist and a determination like the one I had that very night. I was reminded of how I felt then compared to how I'd felt now. How I'd believed no one loved me or would even care that I was gone. How I was tired of being mistreated and wanted to end it all, leaving them, my parents and siblings, to deal with the consequence of mistreating me. And then, I remembered what stopped me; the reason I hadn't gone through with it back then when I stood in the middle of the kitchen. The reminder that I would be sentenced to eternity in hell if I committed suicide popped into my head and forced me to reconsider my plans.

Earlier in my childhood, I had been raised in the Catholic church and been taught about the punitive nature of God. I believe it was during the preparatory classes I took to qualify for my first communion, where I first learned about sin and its consequences, suicide being one of them.

And while I had stopped going to church and practicing that religion, the seeds that had been sown at age eight, were now presenting themselves at age 13. So, there I was, with the knife pressed against the vein in my left arm, ready to put an end to everything in my world, and that thought jumped out at me; "if you commit suicide, you will spend eternity in hell." And at that moment, while I didn't really know God or fully believed He was real, I knew I didn't want to go to hell. So, I put the knife down, went up to my room and cried myself to sleep.

I had bought into the whole religious thing and went to church, and prayed, and believed He would bless me if I was a good person and did good things to and for others.

Twelve years later, here I was in the same position, except this time I was older, in my own apartment, had gotten saved, and had somewhat of a relationship with God. By this time, as I sat on my bed recounting the incident that transpired when I was 13, and the reason I didn't go through with it then, something shifted in me and I decided to have a talk with God. I told Him my plans (not that He didn't already know). I told Him I was done and I didn't want to be in this world anymore if this was what life had to offer me. I was tired of being taken advantage of and treated like crap. I believed the alternative had to be better than what I was experiencing. Actually, it was more of a screaming match at first, as I poured out all that had been weighing heavy on my soul; the sorrow, pain, and regret God allowed me to go through and endure; the hatred I had experienced from those I once cared about; the friendships that had turned out to be fake and the disappointment that came with that; the men (boys) I had given my heart to only to have it rejected and thrown back in my face; the lies, betrayal, and shame I endured at the hands of my cheating boyfriends; and the worst of these, the hole in my heart caused by my family's rejection of me and the belief that my own mother didn't love me.

> *With tears in my eyes, and almost all the hope I had inside of me gone, I told Him that if He was in fact real, to prove it to me and reveal my purpose.*

At some point during the verbal barrage of questions and accusations of God, I slipped off the bed and ended up on the floor crying, hyperventilating, and gasping for air With tears in my eyes, and almost all the hope I had inside of me gone, I told Him that if He was, in fact, real, and didn't want me to move forward with my plans, that I needed Him to prove it to me; to show me my purpose; to help me understand why He would put me on this earth (as described in the Bible), only to suffer and live in a constant state of pain. I went on to share how it would be easier to accept the pain if I knew WHY or could understand the purpose behind it. I had bought into the whole religious thing and went to church, and prayed, and believed He would bless me if I was a good person and did good things to and for others. I had believed the stories about Jesus and how He sacrificed His life for us. I had spent a life believing what my parents, the priests, pastors, and prophets said about Him. Yet, in that very moment, I needed Him to show Himself to me, proving that He was real, and that there was indeed a purpose for being here on this earth…or else, I would take my life and just have to deal with the consequences.

And then, at that moment, it happened. He responded! As I sat there on the floor, with no hope of making it to the end of the week, God Himself, showed up in my bedroom, and wrapped His arms around me. Now, I understand to some people, this might sound crazy or unbelievable, but it's the only way I can describe what took place. I literally felt the warmth and power of His arms wrap around me, and all I could do was sob like a baby as He held me in His arms until I fell asleep. Some people have encounters with angels and can provide similar accounts, but I can tell you without a shadow of a doubt, He presented Himself to me so that I would know without a shadow of a doubt, that not only was

He real, but that He heard me, and that He loved me. I fell asleep that night on the floor in fetal position, waking up the next morning in the same position. By then, I had abandoned my plans to commit suicide and set out on a journey to get to know this God, who revealed Himself to me the night before. I became determined to learn more about my purpose here on earth since I now had a reason to believe that my life was valuable and had a purpose.

He presented Himself to me, so that I would know without a shadow of a doubt, that not only was He real, but that He heard me, and that He loved me.

CHAPTER 2

Getting to the Root

I believed my purpose was contained in the pages of those four gospels, and became obsessed with reading and learning about Jesus' life in hopes of uncovering the truth about my own.

After experiencing that supernatural encounter with God, I rationed in my mind, if I was going to learn more about Him, I needed to learn about Jesus, who was said to be God in human form. So, I spent the next several weeks reading the bible and learning more about Jesus' life, what He said, how He operated here on earth, and the promises He had made. As I read the four gospels about Jesus, I didn't just read it like it was a history book or a bunch of stories. Instead, I read it looking for clues to my identity and purpose here on earth. My request to God had been to reveal my purpose, so I believed my purpose was contained in the pages of those four gospels. I became obsessed with reading and learning about Jesus' life in hopes of uncovering the truth about my own. And though a lot was revealed to me (and continues to be revealed) about Jesus, His character, nature, power, and so on, it wasn't until I came across the story of Joseph, that my entire life's journey began to make sense.

For those unfamiliar with the story of Joseph (found in Genesis 37, 39-50), it takes place before the Israelites are brought into slavery in Egypt. To give a brief synopsis, Joseph was one of 12 sons born to his father. He and his youngest brother shared the same mother, who was the love of their father's life. And because of this, their father showed more affection towards them, especially Joseph, than he did his other ten sons, this of course, made the other brothers jealous of Joseph and hateful towards his existence.

One day, Joseph inadvertently made things worse by sharing a dream he had, where he saw grains of wheat, which represented his brothers, bowing down before him. This clearly angered them, to the point they plotted to kill him. Now, most would wonder, how could a simple dream lead others to become so hateful towards their own flesh and blood? I know firsthand what it is like to witness a parent favoring some children over others, so I can imagine they were simply projecting their pain onto Joseph, but that was the least of Joseph's woes.

In an attempt to carry out their plot to kill him, they threw him into a pit (likened to a deep well) and decided to leave him there for dead. Taking his special coat, which had been gifted to him by his father, they decide to use the coat as evidence for their lie about his death. After some time in the pit, Joseph was dug out and later sold to slave masters by his brothers, who then sold him to the Governor of Egypt.

As a result of his strong leadership and strategic capabilities however, Joseph quickly rose up the ranks and became the Prime Minister of the Governor's affairs and household. He was given free rein and access to make decisions on behalf of the Governor with no questions asked. This is of course until he is accused of sexual assault by the Governor's wife, who lied because he refused to sleep with her. As a result, he is thrown into jail to serve an unfair sentence for a crime he didn't commit.

Fast forward a few years afterward, Joseph is promoted while in prison as the right-hand man to the prison guard and uses his gift of interpreting dreams to bring clarity and understanding to the meaning behind the King's baker and cupbearer's dreams. Back in the day, kings had cupbearers, and their primary role was to taste the wine or drink before the king, in case it had been poisoned. They were essentially taste-testers who risked losing their lives should anything be put into the drink that wasn't supposed to be there. Going back to Joseph, he interprets both dreams with accuracy, resulting in the death of the cupbearer and the reinstatement of the baker. The baker, however, so excited about his parole, ends up forgetting about Joseph's help and goes on about his life.

I'll share more about Joseph's triumphant victory and subsequent vindication in a later chapter, but to wrap up this summary of Joseph's captivating story, the baker eventually remembers what Joseph did for him when the King (Pharaoh) has two disturbing dreams he struggles to understand. The baker then recommends Joseph to the King, and upon Joseph's interpretation and suggested strategy, he is elevated from being a prisoner to the second in command to the King of Egypt. He ends up saving an entire nation from famine (or modern-day economic depression), bringing his family into safety, and fulfilling his life's purpose and God's will.

I know firsthand what it is like to witness a parent favoring some children over others, so I can imagine they were simply projecting their pain onto Joseph.

So, what was it about Joseph's life and story that stood out as a ray of hope for me on my quest to finding my purpose? The answer is simple, yet complicated at the same time. Similar to Joseph, I endured a lot of rejection, pain, and suffering at the hands of my own family. My siblings treated me like crap, especially my oldest brother. He just has an abusive nature about him, even to this day, I don't know the full extent of what happened to him as a child, (and may never really know), but I know for sure he harbors a lot of rage and anger towards others, especially women. I experienced that rage quite often as a young child, who just wanted a brother she could get along with.

I came to the United States with my father at the age of three, and by the time I was about six, my oldest brother had entered the U.S. and was living with us. Things were great in the beginning when he first got here. My other two siblings were still in Haiti, awaiting their paperwork, so for the time being, he was my favorite sibling. But as time went on, the demons in his head started turning against me. I became his punching bag. The slightest aggravation resulted in a beatdown.

There are times I recall getting punched so hard in the chest, that I literally stopped breathing. This became a regular occurrence. There were times where I told my parents, and he simply got yelled at, and other times, where I said nothing, in fear that the retaliation would be much more severe. Aside from being his punching bag, I also became his "tester' aka the one he would test out different sexual acts on. There was never intercourse, but there was certainly enough "inappropriate testing" to qualify as sexual abuse. Even at an early age, I was able to rationalize, when he's "testing," he's not beating me up, so in order to get him to stop hitting me, I would "offer myself up" for testing to avoid the blows. Can you imagine? A six-year-old having to choose between physical or sexual abuse because the latter "didn't hurt" or so I thought! Though there were no physical scars, the mental and emotional ones left their fair share of damage.

This became the perfect set-up for the next cycle of abuse. About the time I was seven, one of my cousins had gotten engaged and was set to be married that same year. Like a traditional Haitian family, everyone was actively engaged in the planning and execution of the big elaborate event, including my mother. Back then, planning for a wedding meant day trips to NYC to look at dresses, purchase food, etc. It also meant that only the grownups could go, and the kids had to stay behind. Since my parents couldn't afford a babysitter, I was often brought to my aunt's house and left alone with my older cousins, who were mostly male. I'm guessing by now you can see where this is going? While I've had to face much of what happened during that time in order to receive healing, there are parts that remain repressed, specifically around how and when I started playing "the game."

As most seven-year-old girls, I admired my older cousins. There was about six to eight years difference between us, so everything they did and said seemed cool to me at the time. Naturally, I wanted to be around them and be like them. And because I was the only girl in the house at times, with nothing to do besides sit in front of the television until my mother got back, I persisted in asking them to play with me, like any annoying seven-year-old does when they're bored. Except, they didn't want to play. They wanted to hang out in their room. So, when I discovered they were in their room watching pornography, I insisted on joining them, not because I wanted to watch, but because I wanted them to pay attention to me. While my mother, aunts, and cousins spent weeks running around town preparing for the wedding, I was getting passed around and experimented on like the girls in the porno movies; this only reinforced the belief that was seeded through my experience with my brother; the only way to get others to acknowledge or be nice to me is to let them have their way with me, both physically and emotionally.

Then came my other two siblings, who entered the U.S. when I was eight. The same thing, the first few months were great. Finally, I had a big sister and a brother who didn't beat me up, call me names, or do disgusting things to my body. However, my sister and I have different mothers, so as tensions rose between her and my mother, her behavior towards me began to change.

My sister and I are seven years apart, so by the time she entered my life again, I was in middle school and she was in high school. Naturally, I wanted to be "grown" just like her and I tried my best to imitate everything she did, wore, and said This was met with insults, calling me fat, ugly, black (as in dark-skinned), pitting my middle brother against me, and the list goes on. And while this might seem like typical sibling rivalry, the truth is, I needed her! I needed her to be the one person in the house I could turn to and share my hurt, or share the details of the abuse I was secretly experiencing right under everybody's nose. I needed someone to turn to, and I wanted it to be her, but because of her challenges with my mother and her own abandonment issues, she wasn't able to respond in the way I needed her to.

Though there were no physical scars, the mental and emotional scars left their fair share of damage.

See, when it came to her boys, my mother believed (and still believes) they could do no wrong, no matter how terrible they treated her or others, but for us girls, we were the epitome of all the things she hated about herself, so there was no way either of us would catch a break. So unfortunately, my sister had to experience the pain of having an "evil stepmother," which she in turn, elected to take out on me. We've grown to develop a good relationship over the years as she's matured, but while growing up, if given the option, I would have definitely elected to not have a sister. It seems harsh to say now, or even think, but back then, she saw me as her competition, instead of the little sister who idolized her and needed her in my corner.

Then there is my middle brother, the one who lost his twin at birth. We're actually the only two of the bunch who have the same parents. My father went on to have four additional children after me, but as far as immediate family goes, he's the only one I actually share the same DNA with. He and I got along relatively well in the beginning. In fact, he used to protect me at times from my older brother and took many hits, for himself and me. But as time passed, his behavior towards me changed as well. Nothing as bad as the other two, but there was definitely some abuse there.

Given what I had experienced, it was no surprise I could relate to Joseph's story, and more importantly, his pain. The things that occurred during my childhood were enough to leave me traumatized or psychologically and emotionally damaged for life. But thankfully, that wasn't God's plan for me! And though the events that brought us to the lowest places of our lives were different, Joseph and I shared a common affliction, called rejection. It would be much later in my walk with God, that I would learn exactly how much of a gift the rejection I faced in my household was. The rejection I faced from my family, and those whom I later welcomed as members of my extended family, would eventually serve as confirmation of who I was and what I had been purposed to do.

CHAPTER 3

Permission to Heal

I came to understand just how much of a painful process the butterfly endure to become such an admired creature.

A few years after beginning my quest to learn more about God and uncover additional details about my purpose, I was led to study the process of transformation, also known as metamorphosis. According to the Merriam-Webster dictionary, metamorphosis is best described as "a change of physical form, structure, or substance especially by supernatural means," with a second definition listed as "a striking alteration in appearance, character, or circumstances." A key synonym for this process is transfiguration. During this period, I also began researching caterpillars and their transformation process into butterflies, in hopes of gaining perspective and understanding of what was taking place inside and around me. It was then that I learned (or relearned) just how uncomfortable the process of metamorphosis really is. Like most people, I used to look at butterflies and see their beauty and majestic nature and think "wow," what an amazing and beautiful creature. To this day, I can't look at a butterfly and not smile and stare in wonder as they fly around spreading their beauty. Well, it wasn't until I did my research that I came to understand just how much of a painful process the butterfly endure to become such an admired creature.

In their caterpillar state, they spend most of their time at the lowest levels of the earth eating and consuming as much as they can. When led, they are elevated from the ground or low place that they've been abiding, only to be ushered into a process which results in a "death" of their former state, completely shedding any resemblance of their old nature. Their insides are completely splattered and turned into a soup-like mush, and they undergo metamorphosis at the cellular level. Can you imagine voluntarily surrendering every part of you, leaving no resemblance behind of your former state, with no real guarantee that you'll be put back together again? Unlike us humans, who avoid change, discomfort and anything that takes away our sense of control and security, they don't fight it or run from it. They simply yield to it, allowing the process designed by their Creator to occur.

Since crying out to God, and asking Him to show Himself to me, I've been in a continual cycle of transformation, except my participation wasn't voluntary, at least not at first. Much like a caterpillar's metamorphosis, which takes place in stages, I've experienced the process of transformation in stages; the first being, my surrender to the complete and total process upon uncovering a hidden truth.

Throughout the last twelve years, God has literally turned my life, my being, and my soul inside out. Experiencing healing one layer at a time, I've gone through what has felt like a long, excruciating process of deliverance and healing, where every single part of me; my thoughts, behavior patterns, emotional responses, aspirations, desires, relationships, associations, etc. have been completely transformed. For over a decade, I have been in a continual cycle of healing, deliverance, transformation, and restoration. If I'm being honest, I've tried to circumvent the process many times. Not because I didn't want to experience the transformation, freedom, and rewards that came with it, but because I didn't always understand what was happening within me. I would either see it as an attack or beat myself up mentally for not being completely healed or "over" whatever painful experience was being brought to the surface.

A perfect illustration of this took place during an earlier stage of metamorphosis in the latter part of 2009 when I began reverting back to my negative behavior patterns as a way of escape. After weeks of being in a state of depression, not really understanding why or how to "snap out of it," I reached out to my pastor, which was something I had never done. At that point however, the emotional aching had become so unbearable, I just couldn't take it anymore.

Unfortunately, I didn't know where it was coming from, so I couldn't even describe it to him or the associate pastor he passed me off to, for them to help me. So, I leveraged my company's EAP program and sought medical help through a therapist, specializing in childhood trauma. My desire at the time was to gain clarity and understanding of where this "sudden" gut-wrenching pain was coming from.

It took only a few sessions before I was telling her about the gang-rape I experienced at the age of seven. As she asked me questions and I shared details about the incidents, I remember being so calm, like I was just having a casual conversation, but in fact, it was the first time I was telling anyone, much less a stranger, what had been done to me. Even as I described what occurred during that period of my life, I never used the "R-word." It was just too much for me then. I wouldn't allow myself to believe that's what happened to me. At that point, it had been 20 years since the incidents, and I still couldn't bring myself to acknowledge or accept that what took place was not my fault and not "okay" because I didn't stop it or tell after the first time it happened.

It wasn't until she asked me the question, "what if you were talking to a 13-year-old mentally challenged girl and she told you the same thing happened to her, would you consider it rape then?" Naturally, my response was "yes," and when asked why, I answered, "because she probably doesn't really understand what's happening to her." My therapist then exclaimed, "Exactly!" Your mental capacity at seven was the same as that of a mentally challenged 13-year-old." She went on to share that even if I didn't stop it, or told an adult right away, it still doesn't mean I wanted it to happen or even understood fully what was taking place. That's when I finally broke down! Twenty years later, I was finally, mentally and emotionally capable of facing the horrible things that had happened to me as a child. There, in the therapist's office, at the age of twenty seven, I was finally able to admit to myself and her, that I had been repeatedly gang-raped by cousins and their friend, at the age of seven. And most importantly, it was not my fault! I didn't ask for it, and I certainly didn't deserve it! With this revelation staring me in the face, I had a choice to make. I could choose to ignore what had been revealed and continue going through life wounded and emotionally unstable, or I could face it, giving myself permission to grieve and release the decades of pain and torment. As hard as it was and as contrary as it seemed, I chose the latter, forgiving myself, my abusers, and my mother, who I had told, but did nothing to console or defend me considering this damaging revelation.

Once the giant band-aid had been ripped off, I was left with a gaping hole in my soul.

As I recall, after a couple of occurrences of playing "the game," I found myself struggling to use the restroom. Frightened that something was wrong with me or that I was pregnant, I shared my secret with my mother, telling her it hurt when I tried to use the restroom. Upon asking me to explain why and what happened, I gave her partial details of what took place at my aunt's house while they were out shopping. As I recall, I was scolded and the boys were confronted but denied it, so they didn't get into any real trouble. I simply wasn't allowed to be at my aunt's house unsupervised or without an adult present from that day on.

I learned then I guess, what happened "wasn't a big deal," and therefore, didn't warrant any emotion. But during that session, it felt like 1 had finally been given the permission I wanted or needed to grieve over what happened, both because my innocence had been taken away from me and because my mother degraded me even more by scolding me and not believing me when I told her what had happened. It would be another 10 years or so before I shared this with another relative since that therapy session.

Naturally, once the giant band-aid had been ripped off, I was left with a gaping hole in my soul. This was a turning point for me and served as the catalyst for the next stage of my metamorphosis. I liken this stage of my journey to the shedding process, which occurs for caterpillars right before the cellular metamorphosis.

With an understanding that my growth and transformation required total exposure and uncovering of prior wounds and areas of emotional instability, I made the decision to trust God, expecting He'd ensure I made it out on the other side. So I dug my heels in, even more, recommitting to reading my bible every day, going to bible study and Sunday school, spending my free time alone at home instead of out with friends, all so I would never again lose sight of what was most important to me, being close to God, and finding and walking in my purpose. These changes in behavior naturally led to changes in my circle and activities. It would take another three and a half years or so of processing, and the healing of deep wounds, before my past turned into a pile of mush, and I could experience the next layer of the transformation process.

I had finally been given the permission I wanted or needed to grieve over what happened

---

CHAPTER 4

Transformational Pressure

〜

To say I had become unrecognizable to those
who knew me prior to the suicide attempt
and the years following is an understatement

While in the cocoon, something referred to as chrysalis forms. Chrysalis is a hard shell that forms around the cocoon as a protective covering while the caterpillar is being "smashed" from the inside out and beginning to take on its new shape and identity. Luckily for me, God had placed me in a ministry that served as my protective layer during that eight-year period. During my time there, I received a great deal of training, deliverance, healing, and equipping for the different phases of transformation I would eventually experience. And though I didn't always enjoy or like just how it was dished out, in the end, it accomplished what God wanted. I became stronger spiritually as I grew emotionally and mentally. To say I had become unrecognizable to those who knew me prior to the suicide attempt, and the years following, is an understatement. Heck, I barely even recognized myself at times, though I didn't always notice the changes immediately. I was often more focused on the pain of the transformation process than the beauty of who I was becoming. From the time I had my encounter with God in the summer of 2007, through the summer of 2013, I went from being a caterpillar (aka a bottom-feeder on land) to willingly submitting myself and my life to undergo the process of metamorphosis, in hopes of one day transforming into the beautifully crafted creature I was created to be.

It wasn't until the latter part of 2013, that I could begin to identify and see the evidence of the transformation taking place within me. To be honest, 2013 was a very painful year for me, especially the first half. During that time, I experienced what I considered to be an intentional act of God to fully break away any resemblance of my former self. I mean every single aspect of my life was tested, and any trace of my old self that surfaced, was literally charred away. Needless to say, it was not a fun period in my life, and certainly not one I look back on fondly. But in the end, it served its purpose by completely destroying my old identity, bringing forth a new commitment in me to endure the process of transformation already in full swing.

At a time when I was more active in church than I had ever been, and more committed to walking with God, doing everything I knew to do as a Christian, I felt farther away from God than I had ever felt. I felt like I was a criminal on trial. In fact, I distinctly remember God telling me that this portion of the process would be public, but I had no idea what it meant at the time, and somewhat disregarded it. That is of course until I began to experience what He really meant by it.

Now, I'm not one to generally believe everyone is against me. And while I admit there was a period in my life where I believed that others only sought to hurt me, this experience was different. I mean it was as if everyone in my life, from the pastors, leaders in the church, the guy I was seeing at the time, and the people at work got a memo about me overnight and woke up the next day ready to condemn me for crimes I didn't know I had committed. Do you want to talk about being tested? Literally every interaction I had for about six months either ended up with me in tears or angry about the way I was being treated. There was no in-between; I was either sad or mad, and for the life of me, I couldn't figure out what I had done to everyone to cause them to turn on me. Furthermore, my ability to hear God had become even more difficult. This made things a hundred times worse, creating much confusion, and tempting me to slip back into old patterns.

I literally found myself in another war against the same demons that had previously hijacked my mind.

What challenged me most about this part of the process, was not just what was happening externally around me, but the internal "voices" that had reappeared and were trying to make their way back into my life, through my mind and my heart. I literally found myself in another war against the same demons that had previously hijacked my mind, to the point they had convinced me to end my life; except this time, by God's grace and His power working in me, they didn't win! They couldn't win. I was stronger, much more stable, and though I was in a dark place emotionally, I knew God and I knew He wouldn't let me die. So, I held on to this truth, and I fought with everything I had, not to surrender. With the absence of help from my spiritual leaders, I held on to the Holy Spirit and fought my away through to the other side. My resolve never to revisit that dark place from 2007 again was so strong, I did all I knew to do and say spiritually to fight off the attacks until finally, I got the reinforcement I needed and succeeded in defeating an old and familiar part of me.

The next stage of the caterpillar's transformation is the developmental phase of their new bodies. Once the chrysalis is formed and hardened, it takes about two weeks for their wings to begin to form and their new shape to develop. From there, they break through and emerge from their protective layer. Though still small and fragile, they literally use the liquid inside of them to pump fluid into their wings until they expand and are strong enough to fly away. My process took much more than two weeks; more like two years, but followed a similar pattern, nonetheless.

My developmental phase began in 2014. By this time, I had gone back to school to get my masters and had grown tremendously in my relationship with God, to the point I could see glimpses of the strength I had developed and the power growing inside of me. I was extremely active in ministry, serving in multiple capacities and growing closer in relationship with the leadership. Workwise, I was excelling in my role and had really become a trusted advisor and coach to the leaders and employees I supported. Admittedly, I had a lot on my plate but didn't notice at first. In fact, I was just so happy to be out of the dark place I'd been in most of my life, that the weight of everything I was juggling didn't seem to matter. This was especially true when it came to ministry.

I was juggling a lot, but it didn't feel as daunting then, as it really was. During that two-year developmental period, I was employed with a smaller company. In the beginning, the role was relatively stress-free, as not a lot of hiring was needed. This gave me the time and flexibility I needed to pursue my masters' degree. The program only required my physical presence once weekly, with online requirements throughout the week. My goal at the time was to complete my degree and use it as leverage to either gain promotion within the organization or shift my focus from being a specialist to moving into a more generalist role within HR. It didn't take long after starting, that I realized there was no room for growth for me at the company, but I decided to stick it out anyway, in hopes things would change when I finally got my degree.

A couple of months into the program, things got really busy, and the company began experiencing record turn-over as a result of key changes in leadership. This meant I went from working just 40 hours a week to 45 and on some weeks, 50 hours. Now, I realize this might be standard for many companies, but this was totally abnormal in this environment. Being the overachiever, I didn't ask for additional help; partly because I believed this was what was expected of me, and because I technically had someone assigned to help, who in my opinion, lacked the competence and motivation to take on more responsibility, so I ended up carrying most of the load. There was even a point, where I'd become so overwhelmed, I had to take a break from school, which was about 8 weeks, just to recover and catch my breath. My determination to finish was strong enough that I went back once the eight weeks were over. However, this meant doubling up on classes later in the year, which only added to my stress, and later became a contributing factor to my breakdown.

Additionally, as a member of a small church, the expectations were pretty high, as far as time commitment and participation in activities go. Spiritually speaking, it was great. I was part of just about every ministry, i.e. dance, prophetic, prayer & intercession, singles, etc., so I learned a ton and grew in my spiritual walk and relationship with God. My relationships with the leaders and other members grew even stronger, with many of us sharing common interests, including fitness and travel. Naturally, they became more like family. In fact, I felt closer to them than I did anyone in my family, so in my mind and in my heart, they had replaced my biological family. Now, that's not to say, everything was rosy and there weren't a few challenging personalities I had to learn to navigate around at times, but all-in-all, they were my family.

As the months went by, the pressure at work, school, and within the ministry intensified greatly. As if that wasn't enough, I decided to add to the chaos by signing up to train and participate in a fitness competition. This of course required additional focus and time on workouts, meal prep, posing, and so on. Funny, as I write this, I keep asking myself "what were you thinking?" Seriously though, as I look back, I'm actually surprised I didn't breakdown sooner! For months leading up to the meltdown, I literally did the same thing every day from the time I woke up at 4:30 am to when I went to bed around 11:00 pm. The weekends were just as crowded and routined, except my day started at 6 am, and instead of an eight-hour workday, I spent five to six hours in church on Sundays. I literally became what felt like a walking zombie, with little time to myself. It was to the point where I stopped taking time out of work, not because I couldn't, but because I felt bad given how busy things were, and I was literally the only one who could do my job.

God-forbid I didn't show up for a ministry-related event or activity, I would have to deal with all the backlash and condemnation from the leadership. To give you an idea of the expectations, I had scheduled to have my wisdom tooth taken out on New Year's Eve one year. I knew I wouldn't be out partying anyway, so it didn't matter that I'd have to stay home. I was a member of the dance team, and during rehearsal the prior week, I announced I wouldn't be at the NYE service due to my surgery. Now mind you, we weren't scheduled to minister anything special that evening, just our regular flow. Shortly following, one of the ministers told me that she understood my situation, but she felt I needed to be at service. So, what did I do? Pumped on pain killers, I planned for someone to pick me up and drop me off at home, and I went to service drowsy, barely able to talk, with a mouth full of cotton balls, soaking up the blood from the surgery. In retrospect, I should have thanked her for her feedback and stayed my behind home, but I was so committed then, it didn't dawn on me just how ridiculous other's expectations were of me.

I believe it was about February or March of 2016 when all the nuts and bolts I had put in place to keep everything together, started coming loose and stuff started hitting the fan. See, it wasn't just my schedule or all the things that were expected of me. The bulk of the weight rested in my inability, or maybe even refusal, to let go of everything I had been trying to hold on to. As I neared my last class, which involved me doing a ton of research and writing for my thesis, the weight had become so unbearable that I couldn't take it anymore and had a meltdown. It just so happened, after dance rehearsal one night, my friend and I were standing in the parking lot talking. I'm not sure what prompted the conversation initially, but I remember just sobbing uncontrollably as I shared with her what was going on in my life. And honestly, up until that moment when I "broke," I didn't even realize how heavy of a load I had been carrying. I was struggling with having to let go of anything that had become part of my protective shell, aka my chrysalis.

After sharing my heart with her, and during my drive home that night, I finally made the decision to take the first step towards my breakthrough; submitting my resignation at work and initiating my transition process. And that's exactly what I did the following morning. Though they did try to get me to stay by creating a new opportunity, I knew in my heart that my time there was done. I had outgrown my protective shell, and any attempt to remain would only cause suffocation, stunted growth, and eventual death because I couldn't access the nutrients I needed to survive.

Once I did that, the weight that had been resting on my chest for months began to lift. This was the first step in a series of "breakups" and breakthroughs that would take place over the course of six weeks. Next came my role as a dance instructor, then came school, which technically was a scheduled breakup, but an ending, nonetheless. Shortly after, came the ending of my on-and-off again relationship. It was a hard decision to follow through on, especially given our history, but I knew in my heart he couldn't come with me on the next leg of my journey, so we parted ways.

I had outgrown my protective shell, and any attempt to remain would only cause suffocation, stunted growth, and eventual death because I couldn't access the nutrients I needed to survive.

Then came the biggest breakup of them all. Given what I've previously shared regarding those in the ministry serving as both my family and "protective shell," you can only imagine how gut-wrenchingly painful it was to have to break away, learning to function in my new body and exercising the use of my wings without them.

CHAPTER 5

Developmental Breakthrough

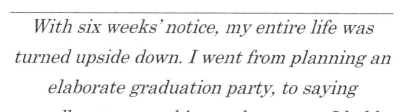

With six weeks' notice, my entire life was turned upside down. I went from planning an elaborate graduation party, to saying goodbye to everything and everyone I held dear to me.

In the mist of all this emotional, mental, and spiritual pressure, and as I neared my final few classes in the program, I began searching for my next role. Finally accepting the fact that another opportunity didn't exist with my then employer, I set out to create a new career path, not knowing this decision would serve as the catalyst for the biggest breakthrough and the deepest pain I have experienced to date. Within a few weeks, I successfully landed a role with a global employer late 2015. However, due to the role's structure, I wasn't slated to start until June of the following year, which at the time, seemed so far away. Therefore, I chose to only share the good news with my pastor, a couple of close friends, including some within the ministry, and my then boyfriend. Afterall, it wasn't something I felt I needed to tell everyone, especially since it was so far away and because I didn't want to jeopardize my current employment, should things "fall through." Additionally, I didn't even have a definitive start date, so there was no way I was going to say much about it to anyone until I had something in writing and had been given the green light from all the pre-employment testing.

By the time March 2016 came around, I had received the details about my start date and choices for my first role. The opportunities were presented in such a way that we were asked to rate our choices based on the role or type of experience we wanted to gain. I rated my choices based on the skills and experience I'd hoped to gain in each assignment, and was convinced nothing about life as I knew it, would change or be impacted. As with previous career decisions, changing jobs didn't seem like a big deal or something I needed to broadcast to everyone. But oh, was I in for a surprise! Following the confirmation of my start date, I was then given six weeks' notice that I would be relocating to Houston, TX for my first assignment. With six weeks' notice, my entire life was turned upside down. I went from planning an elaborate graduation party, to packing, flying down to Houston looking for apartments (which I had never even visited), becoming a landlord, and saying goodbye to everything and everyone I held dear to me.

I knew I had been positioned for growth, but didn't realize my transformation would cost me everyone and everything that helped form the person I'd become up until this phase of my development

---

Unlike previous stages within the transformation process I'd experienced, this one caught me completely off guard. I knew I had been positioned for growth but didn't realize it would cost me everyone and everything that helped form the person I'd become up until this phase of my transformation. In addition to breaking away from those I considered family, I also had to completely break away from everything that was part of my old identity, including my career, my relationship, and some friendships. I had to leave the city I had called home for seven years and the state I had spent most of my life in, since migrating to the U.S.

Though I couldn't articulate it at the time, this part of the process was really hard for me to walk through. In fact, I became so resistant to letting go of the people, places and things that had become part of my protective shell, I literally put my health in danger, almost jeopardizing all the work that had gone into discovering and walking in my purpose and new identity.

This phase of the transformation process taught me a great deal, to say the least. Up until this point, I believed the hardest part of a caterpillar's metamorphosis was the initial cocoon phase, in which their entire form was destroyed and left in a mush-like state. However, after going through my own journey, I realize there is yet an even harder, more painful phase, known as development; the transitional phase between the dying of the old identity and the emergence of the new being.

Before butterflies have even gained their full strength, size, and form, they are required to breakthrough and break out of their hard-protective covering. Their ability to survive and experience life in their new form and capacity, becomes dependent on them piercing through and completely separating from the very thing that served as their protection and covering during their most vulnerable state of existence.

Like the newly formed butterfly, my time in the protective shell was up. This was certainly evidenced in the way I was treated during my transition, both at work and within the ministry. I literally went from being part of a tight-knitted family one day, to feeling like an outsider, an intruder, even in "my own home," both at work and church. It was brutal. So much so, I remained in denial for some time, refusing to believe the same individuals, who'd served as my protective shell, and with whom I had shared my all, had become so cold and unwelcoming. As the threat to my growth became more and more evident, I was faced with a non-retractable decision. I could choose to either remain in the place of comfort and perceived protection or break out, armed with the power and strength gained through God's instructions and confirmation about the next phase of my journey. Needless to say, I chose the latter. Though I might have wanted to avoid the excruciating pain that came with that decision, I have no regrets!

Had my environment remained in a favorable state, I may have never found the courage to explore my new form and state of being.

In choosing to forgo comfort and familiarity, I learned the true cost of growth, the true cost of transformation, and the pain that comes with it. Had either environment remained in a favorable state, I may have never found the courage to explore my new form and state of being. I may have never gained the strength I needed in my "new wings" to explore and fly into new territories. I may have even forfeited the opportunity to soar to new heights and see things from a more expansive vantage point. Now, when I see a butterfly, I still gaze at its majestic beauty, but I'm even more in awe of the process it endured to transform into its new identity.

CHAPTER 6

Courage to Soar

Transformation is a continual process. It never ends. In fact, it only gets more intense the higher you go and the greater your reach

The degree of breakthrough and growth I've experienced since breaking out and away from my "shell", has developed a level of strength and resolve in me that I never believed was possible, especially considering my upbringing and all the things I've come against, in my short time here on earth. In fact, had it not been for the fierceness of the opposition I faced during those vulnerable periods of my life, I wouldn't have made it through the subsequent challenges I've had to overcome during my time of adjustment and exploration in my new identity.

In studying the life of a butterfly, I learned that once enough strength is gained in their wings to fly away, their next stop is usually to find food in the form of nectar, transitioning from the leaves they were previously accustomed to feeding on. In addition to the shift in appetite, they also experience a shift in focus. No longer are they only concerned with consuming as much food as they can, but now their focus is on intimacy and recreating the process for the next generation of caterpillars.

Having emerged from the developmental process with deep wounds of sorrow over the life I'd just shed, along with fear and uncertainty about this new existence, I began my journey of healing and exploration, armed with a new focus, identity, and territory. I won't lie, the previous phase of the journey was gut-wrenchingly painful. I'm not just saying that for the sake of using descriptive language, it literally felt like my soul had been ripped apart by hand, and all that remained was an empty, hollow vacuum. Up until that period, most of the pain I had to process was from the trauma I experienced as a child. Since crying out for hope that dreadful night on my bedroom floor, and outside of dealing with the deaths of my aunt and grandmother, I really hadn't experienced anything "new" or traumatic to that extent. Though I'd gained the strength needed to leave behind my past shell, the initial aftermath left me broken, tired and feeling like a fish out of water.

Initially, I naively expected things to fall in place and all obstacles removed, once the cycle of transformation had occurred, However, as I've painstakingly realized these past few years, transformation is a continual process. Unlike the butterfly, who undergoes a one-time experience in the transformation chamber, the process for us humans never ends. That is of course if we are yielded and have a desire to grow. And truth be told, it only gets more intense the higher you go and the greater your reach. If I've learned anything this past decade, is that the willingness to enter the cocoon and begin the process all over again becomes more and more challenging every time you must do so. Why? Because this time, you know the outcome. You know the level of destruction to your inner being that is about to take place. You know the level of isolation you are about to face and the feelings that come with it. You know the worry and anxiety you'll experience thinking about the outcome and how your new form will turn out. You're well aware of the relationships you'll have to separate from, and the heartache you'll endure as a result. You know the agony and torture of being enclosed in that dark tiny place, created for your protection, but limiting in every way possible. You know what it feels like to gasp for air after expending all your energy to pierce through the darkness for a peek at the light waiting for you on the other side. And though the mere thought of all of these is enough to send most people screaming in the opposite direction, I on the other hand, have learned to accept that all these are a necessary part of growth. Though this knowledge doesn't always make it easier, the excitement of discovery and the expectation of experiencing impact and creating something bigger than myself is enough to keep me going.

The willingness to enter the cocoon and begin the process all over again becomes more and more challenging every time

Experiencing the different phases of change and transformation has become a frequent occurrence for me. The more I've yielded and allowed my hunger to uncover my purpose and reason for being, and driven by my actions, the more I've grown in my thinking, emotions, and spiritual understanding. At this stage of my journey, I can confidently say, every single part of the old me has experienced the process of metamorphosis. Thankfully, it didn't occur all at once, or I might have gone insane in the process.

What started as a decision to shift my career focus, led to a total life makeover that would forever change me, my mindset and outlook on what it means to grow and uncover your hidden beauty and identity. As I've explored life in this new version of myself, I've also been able to explore new parts of this external world, living in four states and having visited two continents. I wholeheartedly believe these experiences were made possible as a result of my obedience and determination to endure the transformation process. These experiences also produced the courage and freedom I needed to continue down the path of uncovering my purpose.

Most recently, I endured yet another round of transformation as I shifted into full-time entrepreneurship. I could write an entirely separate book about that process alone, and probably will one day, but for now, I can assure you the process remained the same and was just as equally grueling as previous times. Though this time, the growth produced seems somehow multiplied and evident in every part of my being, from my thinking, emotional responses, perspective, relationships (especially my relationship with God), and future focus.

As I've transitioned into my career as a Transformational Leader and Coach, I've had the pleasure and honor of meeting many individuals from all walks of life. These individuals vary from business owners and entrepreneurs to corporate professionals, to social change agents, and young adults just starting out on their journey to personal and professional discovery. The thing that fascinates me most about those I've encountered is that they all appear to want the same thing; to find meaning in their work and show up in the best and most impactful way possible for themselves and those around them. I for one think this is a wonderful outlook and one every one of us should strive for throughout our journey here on earth. But the painful reality is, while many want to show up in such honorable and commendable ways, many simply don't ever end up doing so. For some, the lack of direction or know-how becomes the barrier, and for others, the fear of the unknown is enough to stop them cold in their tracks. But for many, it is simply the unwillingness to let go of the old and familiar that keeps them in this perpetual state of hoping and wishing. That place where "someday" takes the front seat and their dreams, aspirations, and life's purpose takes the back seat. This is understandable, and I can certainly empathize considering my first-hand knowledge of just how intense, invasive, and unnerving the process of transformation can be. However, the truth remains, in order to see and experience massive growth in our personal lives and the world around us, our only option is to let go and give ourselves permission to become the version of us we want to see. The "us" we want the world to see. The "us" the generations behind us are waiting to see step up.

CHAPTER 7

Purpose Revealed

> *I've come to understand that my metamorphosis wasn't just about me.*

As I wrap up this phase of my transformational journey, God has led me back to Joseph's story to see beyond the pain and suffering he endured. With fresh eyes and a new perspective, I can relate to him and his story even more because of his redemption, and that of his family. In the latter part of the story, we see that things not only turned around for Joseph, but he was vindicated of every accusation and form of abuse he had endured and experienced reconciliation with his family.

Once Joseph was elevated to the second highest seat in the King's palace, he became an instrumental resource in Egypt, managing the gross domestic product (GDP) wisely and efficiently. His ability to manage the nation's resources, in what was considered the worst recession the country and other neighboring nations had experienced, opened the door for redemption and reconciliation. As a result of the recession (which the bible refers to as a famine), Joseph's brothers were forced to seek food from Egypt, the only nation with resources. When they got there, they found much more than they had expected. They found the brother they had abused and once left for dead, operating as the King's Chief of Staff and ruling over all the nation's resources.

His life had become so unrecognizable, his brothers didn't know who he was at first. They just saw him as the authority figure that he had become. And while Joseph did his fair share of testing them to see if they were the same callous people who threw him in the pit out of hate and jealousy, he eventually welcomed them back into his life with open arms, once he saw they had changed. As you can imagine, this must have left Joseph's brothers dumbfounded, remorseful, and even a little scared of what he would or could do as payback. And though no one would have thought Joseph wrong for putting them to death, or giving orders to inflict torture, that's not what he did at all. Instead, he welcomed them back into his life with open arms and made provision for them to come and live with him and his family in Egypt.

As I've shared, I initially resonated with Joseph because of his pain, mostly because I was in pain myself when I first heard of him and his experiences. I was just beginning to heal from the abuse that took place during my childhood, and Joseph's vindication became an anchor and what I wanted to see happen most in my life. But over the course of the last three years, things have shifted greatly for me. Since breaking free and separating from all the people, places, and things, which constituted my old identity, my entire perspective has shifted. Where I so desperately wanted vindication and payback, I've transitioned to praying for healing and restoration. Where I once despised certain situations and adversities, I've shifted to looking for the lessons and growth opportunities. I've come to understand that my metamorphosis wasn't just about me, at least not completely. My experiences as a child, adolescent, and even as an adult, were all hand-crafted and selected for me by God. Not because I was hated or being punished, but because I had been chosen for the purpose of being used as a vessel to help bring others into a place of healing and restoration, including my family.

You see, what I haven't yet shared, and what was only revealed to me as I began the process of writing this book, was that I had come from a long line of abuse of varying capacities. The stories I've shared about what happened to me aren't mine alone. In fact, they represent the stories of many women in my family, who for one reason or another, have never shared what they've been through, and have never seized the opportunity to step outside the shadows of pain, guilt, and shamc to reveal their truth. For generations, they were told they had to grin and bear it, and for decades, that's exactly what they did. My mother, as mean and as hurtful as she has been towards me, shares a similar story. In fact, this is the irony of all of this.

The stories I've shared about what happened to me aren't mine alone. In fact, they represent the stories of many

---

As a child, I truly believed she hated me. As I've matured in age and spiritually, I've come to understand that it is not hatred that I've experienced, but rather an inability to love, stemming from her own experiences of pain and suffering. Unsurprisingly, she had a tumultuous relationship with her mother, my grandmother. Though she rarely talks about her childhood, the few things she has recounted, have all centered around my grandmother's abuse towards her and the preferential treatment of her brothers, my uncles. So, it should have been no surprise to me this was the pattern of behavior she followed when it came to her own children. History had in fact, repeated itself.

I recall being told years back by one of my aunts that my mother's father, who she never talks about and barely even knows, is a first cousin to my grandmother, which makes her a product of incest. When I first learned of this, I was about fourteen years old and was shocked, but I never asked her about it out of fear she might retaliate against my aunt or me. I've always kept it in mind, wondering if this was the reason behind my grandmother's harsh dealings with her. Perhaps my grandmother only saw my mother as the object of her shame, and therefore rejected her, sowing the seeds that would later lead my mother to reject me. And though my mother has never shared this with me directly, I suspect she too, was the victim of sexual abuse. I don't have definite proof, but as I've replayed her response, considering what I told her had been done to me at the young age of seven, I can't imagine that she hadn't experienced the same atrocities.

As I've come to these revelations about the women in my family, specifically my grandmother and mother, my heart is grieved. And even as I think about the generations of young men who committed these horrible acts, I find myself feeling sympathy towards them above anything else. This is not because I agree or condone their actions, but because I understand spiritually, they too were under attack. The entire lineage had been infected somewhere down the line and every generation seemed condemned to walk in this sin. That is of course until I came along.

My journey towards transformation began that day I cried out to God asking Him to reveal Himself and my purpose *to me*. It has taken twelve years, but I can finally see the manifested answer to my requests. Initially, I thought my answer had come when I felt His arms wrap around me, there on my bedroom floor. But being the amazing God that He is, He instead chose to reveal Himself, and my purpose, *in me*. What do I mean by this? As I recounted all I'd been through; every experience, every battle, and every struggle I'd endured from my earliest memories back in Haiti, to my present circumstances here in the U.S., I began to connect the dots, uncovering the many ways God had used me and my purpose to break the patterns of abuse and violence that had plagued my family for generations.

The entire lineage had been infected
somewhere down the line and every
generation seemed condemned to walk in this
sin; that is of course until I came along...

One by one, from disease, to mental illness, to idolatry and witchcraft, to emotional bondage and despondency, to poverty, and the biggest of them all, sexual abuse, He's revealed the areas in which I've been used to overcome or break through the things, which haunted the generations before me. My commitment to follow God and trust Him to reveal my purpose, resulted in the revelation of my true identity.

When I cried out that night in search of purpose, I was broken and on the verge of suicide, literally having planned to exit this earth the following day. At that moment, I had absolutely no hope of seeing another complete day, let alone sitting here writing my life's story. This journey through transformation hasn't at all been easy. In fact, it's been the loneliest, most heartbreaking period of my life, but it was all for this purpose; that I would not only come to know God and believe that He is real, but that I would also come into the knowledge of my true identity and purpose in life.

I now have a better understanding as to why things have happened in the manner and timing they did. What has often felt like a weight or burden of pain, was the weight of the injustices endured by generations before me. I didn't die that night because my life mattered. Though I didn't know it then, I know now what my purpose is and how every experience leading up to this point played a role in my process of discovery.

Much of what I've shared about my journey has never been shared with anyone close to me, much less the general public But in obedience to God and in light of the #MeToo movement, I realize I'm not as alone as I was led to believe. Many women and men today suffer violence in the form of physical and sexual abuse and are either shamed or guilted into silence. This book is written as a declaration of hope and freedom for all those who are bound by the wickedness of the generations before them. Those who suffer silently behind guilt, shame, rejection, abandonment, depression, and despair. Those whose circumstances have caused them to believe they are unlovable, unworthy, or undeserving of joy and happiness. Those tired of having to numb their pain with substances, people, and things that leave them feeling even more empty and alone. Those whose hope has been snuffed out by the trials and injustices of life. Those who simply want to know and experience a life outside of pain. Those desperately seeking the answer to the questions; "why am I here?" and "what is my purpose?" To you I say, though it may seem dark or even dim in your world right now, trust and know that if you call on God, He will show up and rescue you. But more importantly, He can and will transform you, revealing your purpose and the beauty hidden inside of you.

Recovery Restoration, *Healing Deliverance*

Freedom Decree

Set Free. From Brokeness

If you have seen parts of yourself in my story and journey, and desire to receive healing for yourself and/or your family, I invite you to pray this decree out loud.

Father in the name of Jesus. I reverence you Lord, in all your glory and in all your splendor. You are the Lord of grace and Lord over Heaven and earth. I bless your holy name, for you are truly worthy of all praise and all honor. You are Alpha and Omega, the beginning and the end. You see to it that ALL things work together for those whom you have created. For those whom you have established in the earth and call your children.

I thank you Holy Spirit for all that you have revealed in my bloodline and lineage. I thank you Holy Spirit for all that you have revealed about me and my identity. I thank you, Father, that you have heard my cries and have seen the things

committed against me. The pain I've endured. The dark valleys I've had to walk through. The places in which I have been weakened.

I thank you, King of Glory, that in spite of what I've dealt with and in spite of what I've been through and experienced, that you still love me. You still favor me. You are still healing me. You are still delivering me in the name of Jesus.

Father, I stand in the gap for my entire bloodline as I declare a release in the name of Jesus, and establish new decrees for me and my family.

Where there's been sin in my bloodline, I release a decree of cleansing and healing in the name of Jesus.

Where there was abandonment in my bloodline, Father I declare, that I am a child of the Most-High God, and joint-heir to the throne with Christ Jesus.

Where rejection plagued me, Father, I come into the acceptance of your love, and sonship in the name of Jesus.

Where pain haunted me and taunted me, and tried to take my life from me, I release a decree of healing, restoration, peace, and joy in the name of Jesus.

Where sexual immorality and sexual sin entered into my bloodline with the distinct assignment to destroy me and my family, I release a decree of purity, holiness, and righteousness in the name of Jesus.

Where fear, guilt, and shame, has created distance and distrust between me and my family, let there be healing and reconciliation in the name of Jesus.

I establish a new covenant this day with the King of Glory.

I cancel out every demonic decree released over me and my family in the name of Jesus, and I replace it with a decree of freedom over me and my family.

I decree in the name of Jesus that every sin is washed clean. That every offense is brought before you in remorse and repentance in the name of Jesus.

I renounce any agreements with idolatry and witchcraft spirits in the name of Jesus.

I override the previous decree of poverty, declaring it has no place, no authority or legal right to function, nor be present anywhere in my bloodline in the name of Jesus.

Let every violent, vicious, despicable, and vile assailant be brought to justice and judgment, causing them to pay seven-fold what they've stolen from me and my family.

And I decree and declare that from this day forward, from this generation forward, that we belong to, walk with, and stand with the King of Glory.

Let our lives become unrecognizable Father, that those who knew us, will know us no more.

Let there be a revealing of our new identity in you to those who knew us in our old form and old garments of bondage.

Let there be a complete unveiling of your glory, of your power, of your healing, of your manifested grace, and identity in me Father.

In the name of Jesus, I am new. I am changed. I am transformed. I am renewed. I am healed. I am delivered. I am set free.

And it is in your Son's name that I seal these decrees. And it is so in Jesus' name. Amen!

About the Author

Sabine Gedeon is the Founder and CEO of Empowered By Purpose. She serves as the Chief Transformation Officer, offering Coaching & Consulting services to ambitious, mission-driven leaders. Having faced several major life transitions and undergoing a series of personal and spiritual transformations, Sabine came to the realization that those who she'd been called to serve needed a deeper level of support. The kind of support that not only gave them the practical and tactical tools they need to advance in life, but also helped them uncover and address the internal barriers keeping them from fully stepping into the person they were created to be.

With over 14 years' experience serving as an HR professional, Coach and Advisor to leaders in Fortune 100 companies, and within her own practice, Sabine' has helped hundreds of professionals breakthrough barriers, uncover or build their leadership capabilities, and experience growth in their lives, careers, and businesses.

Sabine knows first-hand the amount of faith and courage it takes to break away from the norm and step into something new or bigger than yourself. Using her personal experience as a benchmark, she hopes to help lead millions of others through their unique paths of purpose, impact, prosperity, and legacy.

Stay Connected

Thank you for purchasing Transformed, The Journey to Becoming. Sabine would like to connect with you. Below are a few ways you can stay up-to-date on speaking engagements, workshops, new book releases, and more!

Website: www.SabineGedeon.com

LinkedIn: SabineGedeon

Facebook: SabineGedeonCoaching

Instagram: SabineGedeon

Made in the USA
Coppell, TX
11 January 2023

10936008R00056